Presented To:

Jenny + Robert

Presented By:

Nana Gardner

Date:

June 8, 2001

God's Little Book
of Promises

Honor Books
Tulsa, Oklahoma

3rd Printing

God's Little Book of Promises
ISBN 1-56292-496-6
Copyright © 1998 by Honor Books
P.O. Box 55388
Tulsa, Oklahoma 74155

References

Introduction

God has promised His children many things, including His ever present love, forgiveness and faithfulness. His Word is filled with the promises He has made us. *God's Little Book of Promises* explores God's promises on many issues facing us today.

Whether you are struggling spiritually, looking for a way to encourage a friend, or seeking deeper scriptural understanding, you are sure to find a category or scripture that speaks to your heart. While the world tells us one thing about success, family, temptation, joy, and other issues, the Bible often has some different answers. The topical arrangement of *God's Little Book of Promises* provides quick reference to the truths of God's Word so you can find the truth just when you need it.

God is faithful to His Word and eager to bring it to fullness in our lives. This book is designed to start us on the way and to keep us on the path.

Table of Contents

The Truth about Anger

He who is slow to anger has great
understanding, but he who is
quick-tempered exalts folly.
Proverbs 14:29 NASB

He that is slow to anger is better
than the mighty; and he that ruleth
his spirit than he that taketh a city.
Proverbs 16:32 KJV

Wherefore, my beloved brethren,
let every man be swift to hear,
slow to speak, slow to wrath:
For the wrath of man worketh
not the righteousness of God.
James 1:19-20 KJV

For we know him that hath said,
Vengeance belongeth unto me,
I will recompense, saith the Lord.
And again, The Lord shall
judge his people.
Hebrews 10:30 KJV

What To Do When You Are Angry

Be ye angry, and sin not: let not the
sun go down upon your wrath.
Ephesians 4:26 KJV

A soft answer turneth away wrath: but
grievous words stir up anger.
Proverbs 15:1 KJV

For if you forgive men their
trespasses, your heavenly
Father will also forgive you.
Matthew 6:14 NKJV

If it is possible, as much
as depends on you,
live peaceably with all men.
Romans 12:18 NKJV

How To Overcome Improper Anger

But now ye also put off all these;
anger, wrath, malice, blasphemy, filthy
communication out of your mouth.
Colossians 3:8 KJV

Cease from anger, and forsake wrath:
fret not thyself in any wise to do evil.
Psalm 37:8 KJV

Finally, brethren, whatsoever things
are true, whatsoever things are
honest, whatsoever things are just,
whatsoever things are pure,
whatsoever things are lovely,
whatsoever things are of good report,
if there be any virtue, and if there be
any praise, think on these things.
Philippians 4:8 KJV

Accept one another, then, just as
Christ accepted you, in order to
bring praise to God.
Romans 15:7

The Truth about Assurance

I, even I, am he who blots out
your transgression, for my own sake,
and remembers your sins no more.
Isaiah 43:25

As far as the east is from the west,
So far has He removed our
transgressions from us.
Psalm 103:12 NKJV

All that the Father giveth me shall
come to me; and him that cometh
to me I will in no wise cast out.
John 6:37 KJV

Truly, truly, I say to you, he who hears
My word, and believes Him who sent
Me, has eternal life,
and does not come into judgment,
but has passed out of death into life.
John 5:24 NASB

Doubting Your Assurance

For by grace you have been saved through faith; and this not of your own doing, it is the gift of God.
Ephesians 2:8 RSV

And I am sure that God who began the good work within you will keep right on helping you grow in his grace until his task within you is finally finished.
Philippians 1:6 TLB

My sheep hear my voice, and I know them, and they follow me: And I give unto them eternal life; and they shall never perish, neither shall any man pluck them out of my hand.
John 10:27-28 KJV

Let us draw near with a true heart in full assurance of faith, having our hearts sprinkled from an evil conscience and our bodies washed with pure water.
Hebrews 10:22 NKJV

How To Have Assurance

If you confess with your mouth,
"Jesus is Lord," and believe in your
heart that God raised him from
the dead, you will be saved.
Romans 10:9

In Him you also trusted, after you
heard the word of truth, the gospel
of your salvation; in whom also,
having believed, you were sealed
with the Holy Spirit of promise, who
is the guarantee of our inheritance
until the redemption of the purchased
possession, to the praise of His glory.
Ephesians 1:13-14 NJKV

Now He who establishes us with you
in Christ and anointed us is God,
who also sealed us and gave us
the Spirit in our hearts as a pledge.
2 Corinthians 1:21-21 NASB

The Truth about Burdens

Do not be anxious about anything,
but in everything, by prayer and
petition, with thanksgiving, present
your requests to God. And the peace
of God, which transcends all
understanding, will guard
your hearts and your minds
in Christ Jesus.
Philippians 4:6-7

The Lord preserveth the simple: I
was brought low, and he helped me.
Return unto thy rest, O my soul; for
the Lord hath dealt bountifully with
thee. For thou hast delivered my soul
from death, mine eyes from tears,
and my feet from falling.
Psalm 116:6-8 KJV

God's Little Book of Promises

Comfort for Your Burdens

You therefore must endure hardship
as a good soldier of Jesus Christ.
2 Timothy 2:3 NKJV

My brethren, count it all joy
when you fall into various trials.
James 1:2 NKJV

For I, the Lord your God, hold your
right hand; it is I who say to you,
"Fear not, I will help you."
Isaiah 41:13 RSV

These things I have spoken unto you,
that in me ye might have peace.
In the world ye shall have tribulation:
but be of good cheer;
I have overcome the world.
John 16:33 KJV

What To Do about Burdens

Cast thy burden upon the Lord,
and he shall sustain thee.
Psalm 55:22 KJV

Come to me, all you who are weary
and burdened, and I will give you
rest. Take my yoke upon you and
learn from me, for I am gentle and
humble in heart, and you will find
rest for your souls. For my yoke is
easy and my burden is light.
Matthew 11:28-30

Therefore humble yourselves under
the mighty hand of God, that He may
exalt you in due time, casting all your
care upon Him, for He cares for you.
1 Peter 5:6-7 NKJV

Carry each other's burdens,
and in this way you will
fulfill the law of Christ.
Galatians 6:2

The Truth about Careers

I will instruct you and teach
you in the way you should go;
I will guide you with My eye.
Psalm 32:8 NKJV

Without counsel plans go wrong,
but with may advisers they succeed.
Proverbs 15:22 RSV

The purpose in a man's mind is
like deep water, but a man of
understanding will draw it out.
Proverbs 20:5 RSV

For I know the plans I have for you,
says the Lord. They are plans for
good and not for evil, to give
you a future and a hope.
Jeremiah 29:11 TLB

How To Work

Work hard and cheerfully at all you
do, just as though you were working
for the Lord and not merely for
your masters, remembering that it
is the Lord Christ who is going
to pay you, giving you your full
portion of all he owns. He is the
one you are really working for.
Colossians 3:23-24 TLB

For even when we were with you,
we gave you this rule: "If a man
will not work, he shall not eat."
2 Thessalonians 3:10

Now if anyone builds on this
foundation with gold, silver, precious
stones, wood, hay, straw, each one's
work will become clear; for the Day
will declare it, because it will be
revealed by fire; and the fire will test
each one's work, of what sort it is.
1 Corinthians 3:12-13 NKJV

Work from God

As for every man to whom God has
given riches and wealth, and given
him power to eat of it, to receive his
heritage and rejoice in his labor—
this is the gift of God.
Ecclesiastes 5:19 NKJV

Do not labor for the food which
perishes, but for the food which
endures to everlasting life, which
the Son of Man will give you.
John 6:27 NKJV

God is not unjust; he will not forget
your work and the love you have
shown him as you have helped his
people and continue to help them.
Hebrews 6:10

The Truth about Children

The promise is for you and
your children and for all who
are far off—for all whom
the Lord our God will call.
Acts 2:39

But when Jesus saw what was
happening he was very much
displeased with his disciples and
said to them, "Let the children
come to me, for the Kingdom
of God belongs to such as they.
Don't send them away!"
Mark 10:14 TLB

Children are a gift from God; they
are his reward. Children born to a
young man are like sharp arrows to
defend him. Happy is the man who
has his quiver full of them.
Psalm 127:3-5 TLB

Disciplining Children

Train a child in the way
he should go, and when he is
old he will not turn from it.
Proverbs 22:6

He who spares the rod hates his son,
but he who loves him
is diligent to discipline him.
Proverbs 13:24 RSV

Discipline your son, for in that
there is hope; do not be
a willing party to his death.
Proverbs 19:18

Parents and Children

Children, obey your parents in the
Lord: for this is right. Honour thy
father and mother; which is the first
commandment with promise; That
it may be well with thee, and thou
mayest live long on the earth.
Ephesians 6:1-3 KJV

Children, obey your parents
in all things, for this is well
pleasing to the Lord.
Colossians 3:20 NKJV

Only take heed to yourself,
and diligently keep yourself,
lest you forget the things your
eyes have seen, and lest they depart
from your heart all the days of
your life. And teach them to your
children and your grandchildren.
Deuteronomy 4:9 NKJV

The Truth about Comfort

Blessed be the God and Father of
our Lord Jesus Christ, the Father of
mercies and God of all comfort;
who comforts us in all our affliction
so that we may be able to comfort
those who are in any affliction with
the comfort with which we ourselves
are comforted by God.
2 Corinthians 1:3-4 NASB

But the Comforter, which is the
Holy Ghost, whom the Father will
send in my name, he shall teach
you all things, and bring all things
to your remembrance, whatsoever
I have said unto you.
John 14:26 KJV

The Lord is good, a refuge in
times of trouble. He cares for
those who trust in him.
Nahum 1:7

When You Need Comfort

Come to me, all who labor and are
heavy laden, and I will give you rest.
Matthew 11:28 RSV

The Lord is a stronghold for
the oppressed, a stronghold
in times of trouble.
Psalm 9:9 RSV

Though I am surrounded by
troubles, you will bring me safely
through them. You will clench your
fist against my angry enemies!
Your power will save me.
Psalm 138:7 TLB

Don't be impatient. Wait for the
Lord, and he will come and save you!
Be brave, stouthearted and
courageous. Yes, wait and
he will help you.
Psalm 27:14 TLB

God's Little Book of Promises

The Presence of Comfort

For as the sufferings of Christ
abound in us, so our consolation
also abounds through Christ.
2 Corinthians 1:5 NKJV

Cast your cares on the Lord and
he will sustain you; he will never
let the righteous fall.
Psalm 55:22

For the Angel of the Lord guards
and rescues all who reverence him.
Psalm 34:7 TLB

Through the Lord's mercies
we are not consumed, because
His compassions fail not. They are
new every morning; great is
Your faithfulness. "The Lord is
my portion," says my soul,
"Therefore I hope in Him!"
Lamentations 3:22-24 NKJV

The Truth about Commitment

As you therefore have received
Christ Jesus the Lord, so walk in
Him, rooted and built up in Him
and established in the faith,
as you have been taught,
abounding in it with thanksgiving.
Colossians 2:6-7 NKJV

Therefore being justified by faith,
we have peace with God through
our Lord Jesus Christ.
Romans 5:1 KJV

For God hath not appointed us
to wrath, but to obtain salvation
by our Lord Jesus Christ.
1 Thessalonians 5:9 KJV

But we are bound to give thanks
alway to God for you, brethren
beloved of the Lord, because God
hath from the beginning chosen you
to salvation through sanctification of
the Spirit and belief of the truth.
2 Thessalonians 2:13 KJV

Commit Yourself

Commit your way to the Lord,
trust also in Him, and He shall bring
it to pass. He shall bring forth your
righteousness as the light, and
your justice as the noonday.
Psalm 37:5-6 NKJV

Therefore let those who suffer
according to the will of God commit
their souls to Him in doing good,
as to a faithful Creator.
1 Peter 4:19 NKJV

Let your heart therefore be loyal
to the Lord our God, to walk in
His statutes and keep His
commandments, as at this day.
1 Kings 8:61 NKJV

Benefits of Commitment

Ye are washed, but ye are sanctified,
but ye are justified in the name of
the Lord Jesus, and by the
Spirit of our God.
1 Corinthians 6:11 KJV

Commit your work to the Lord,
then it will succeed.
Proverbs 16:3 TLB

Commit everything you do
to the Lord. Trust him to help you
do it and he will. Your innocence
will be clear to everyone. He will
vindicate you with the blazing light
of justice shining down as
from the noonday sun.
Psalm 37:5-6 TLB

The Truth about Conflict

I appeal to you, brethren,
by the name of our Lord Jesus Christ,
that all of you agree and that there
be no dissensions among you,
but that you be united in the
same mind for the same judgment.
1 Corinthians 1:10 RSV

And the Lord's servant must
not quarrel; instead, he
must be kind to everyone,
able to teach, not resentful.
2 Timothy 2:24

A wrathful man stirs up strife,
but he who is slow to anger
allays contention.
Proverbs 15:18 NKJV

How To Avoid Conflict

How good and pleasant it is when
brothers live together in unity!
Psalm 133:1

May the God of steadfastness and
encouragement grant you to live
in such harmony with one another,
in accord with Christ Jesus, that
together you may with one voice
glorify the God and Father
of our Lord Jesus Christ.
Romans 15:5 RSV

Try always to be led along
together by the Holy Spirit, and
so be at peace with one another.
Ephesians 4:3 TLB

And above all these things
put on charity, which is
the bond of perfectness.
Colossians 3:14 KJV

How To Deal with Conflict

Dare any of you, having
a matter against another, go to law
before the unrighteous, and
not before the saints?
1 Corinthians 6:1 NKJV

See that no one repays another
with evil for evil, but always seek
after that which is good for
one another and for all men.
1 Thessalonians 5:15 NASB

Don't grumble about each other,
brothers. Are you yourselves
above criticism? For see!
The great Judge is coming.
James 5:9 TLB

The Truth about Courage

Be of good courage, and he shall
strengthen your heart, all ye
that hope in the Lord.
Psalm 31:24 KJV

Be strong and courageous, do not
fear or be dismayed because of the
king of Assyria, nor because of all the
multitude which is with him;
for the one with us is greater
than the one with him.
2 Chronicles 32:7-8 NASB

Yes, be bold and strong! Banish fear
and doubt! For remember, the Lord
your God is with you wherever you go.
Joshua 1:9 TLB

Peace I leave with you; My peace
I give to you; not as the world gives,
do I give to you. Let not your heart
be troubled, nor let it be fearful.
John 14:27 NASB

When You Need Courage

Wait for the Lord; be strong,
and let your heart take courage;
Yes, wait for the Lord.
Psalm 27:14 NASB

And so we should not be like
cringing, fearful slaves, but we should
behave like God's very own children,
adopted into the bosom of his family,
and calling to him, "Father, Father."
Romans 8:15 TLB

The Lord is my light and my
salvation; whom shall I fear? When
evil men come to destroy me, they
will stumble and fall! Yes, though a
mighty army marches against me,
my heart shall know no fear! I am
confident that God will save me.
Psalm 27:1-3 TLB

Courage from the Father

He gives power to the tired and
worn out, and strength to the weak.
Isaiah 40:29 TLB

Do not fear, little flock, for it is
your Father's good pleasure
to give you the kingdom.
Luke 12:32 NKJV

For I am the Lord, your God, who
takes hold of your right hand and says
to you, Do not fear; I will help you.
Isaiah 41:13

That is why we can say without any
doubt or fear, "The Lord is my Helper
and I am not afraid of anything
that mere man can do to me."
Hebrews 13:6 TLB

Overwhelming victory is
ours through Christ who
loved us enough to die for us.
Romans 8:37 TLB

The Truth about Death

O Death, where is your sting?
O Hades, where is your victory?
1 Corinthians 15:55 NKJV

When calamity comes, the wicked
are brought down, but even in death
the righteous have a refuge.
Proverbs 14:32

Truly, truly, I say to you,
if anyone keeps My word
he will never see death.
John 8:51 NASB

I will ransom them from the
power of the grave; I will redeem
them from death.
Hosea 13:14 KJV

Whoever believes in Him should
not perish but have eternal life.
John 3:15 NKJV

Christ's Death

And since by his blood he did all
this for us as sinners, how much
more will he do for us now that
he has declared us not guilty?
Now he will save us from
all of God's wrath to come.
Romans 5:9 TLB

Since we, God's children, are human
beings—made of flesh and blood—
he became flesh and blood too by
being born in human form; for only
as a human being could he die and
in dying break the power of the devil
who had the power of death.
Hebrews 2:14 TLB

He will swallow up death forever,
and the Lord God will wipe away
tears from all faces; the rebuke of
His people He will take away
from all the earth.
Isaiah 25:8 NKJV

Believers and Death

But God will ransom my soul
from the power of Sheol, for
he will receive me.
Psalm 49:15 RSV

But the good man—what a different
story! For the good man—the
blameless, the upright, the man
of peace—he has a wonderful
future ahead of him. For him
there is a happy ending.
Psalm 37:37 TLB

For to me, to live is Christ
and to die is gain.
Philippians 1:21

The Truth about Deliverance

Because he cleaves to me in love,
I will deliver him; I will protect him,
because he knows my name. When
he calls to me, I will answer him;
I will be with him in trouble,
I will rescue him and honor him.
Psalm 91:14-15 RSV

For he has rescued us out of the
darkness and gloom of Satan's
kingdom and brought us into
the Kingdom of his dear Son.
Colossians 1:13 TLB

The Lord knoweth how to deliver
the godly out of temptations, and
to reserve the unjust unto the day
of judgment to be punished.
2 Peter 2:9 KJV

How To Receive Deliverance

When the righteous cry for help,
the Lord hears, and delivers them
out of all their troubles.
Psalm 34:17 RSV

God blesses those who are kind
to the poor. He helps them
out of their troubles.
Psalm 41:1 TLB

He who trusts in his own heart
is a fool, but whoever walks
wisely will be delivered.
Proverbs 28:26 NKJV

Call to me and I will answer you, and
will tell you great and hidden things
which you have not known.
Jeremiah 33:3 RSV

The Deliverer

The Lord is my rock,
my fortress and my deliverer.
2 Samuel 22:2

The Lord is my rock and my
fortress and my deliverer; my God,
my strength, in whom I will trust;
my shield and the horn of
my salvation, my stronghold.
Psalm 18:2 NKJV

But I am poor and needy;
yet the Lord thinks upon me.
You are my help and my deliverer;
do not delay, O my God.
Psalm 40:17 NKJV

Gracious is the Lord, and righteous;
our God is merciful. The Lord
preserves the simple; when I
was brought low, he saved me.
Psalm 116:5-6 RSV

God's Little Book of Promises

The Truth about Discipline

But I keep under my body, and bring
it into subjection: lest that by any
means, when I have preached to
others, I myself should be a castaway.
1 Corinthians 9:27 KJV

I have been crucified with Christ;
it is no longer I who live, but Christ
lives in me; and the life which I now
live in the flesh I live by faith in
the Son of God, who loved me
and gave Himself for me.
Galatians 2:20 NKJV

He that hath no rule over his own
spirit is like a city that is broken
down, and without walls.
Proverbs 25:28 KJV

How To Have Discipline

Therefore do not let sin reign in your mortal body so that you obey its evil desires. Do not offer the parts of your body to sin, as instruments of wickedness, but rather offer yourselves to God, as those who have been brought from death to life; and offer the parts of your body to him as instruments of righteousness.
Romans 6:12-13

Now your attitudes and thoughts must all be constantly changing for the better. Yes, you must be a new and different person, holy and good. Clothe yourself with this new nature.
Ephesians 4:23-24 TLB

Let us walk properly, as in the day, not in revelry and drunkenness, not in lewdness and lust, not in strife and envy. But put on the Lord Jesus Christ, and make no provision for the flesh, to fulfill its lusts.
Romans 13:13-14 NKJV

Discipline from God

Blessed is the man whom God
corrects; so do not despise the
discipline of the Almighty.
Job 5:17

Blessed is the man whom
Thou dost chasten, O Lord,
and dost teach out of Thy Law.
Psalm 94:12 NASB

"I am with you and will save you,"
declares the Lord. "Though I
completely destroy all the nations
among which I scatter you, I will
not completely destroy you. I will
discipline you but only with justice."
Jeremiah 30:11

As many as I love, I rebuke
and chasten. Therefore be
zealous and repent.
Revelation 3:19 NKJV

45

The Truth about Discontentment

All the days of the afflicted are evil,
But he who is of a merry heart
has a continual feast.
Proverbs 15:15 NKJV

Now godliness with
contentment is great gain.
1 Timothy 6:6 NKJV

Let not thine heart envy sinners:
but be thou in the fear of the Lord
all the day long. For surely there is
an end; and thine expectation
shall not be cut off.
Proverbs 23:17-18 KJV

Seek the Lord and his strength,
seek his face continually.
Remember his marvellous works
that he hath done, his wonders,
and the judgments of his mouth.
1 Chronicles 16:11-12 KJV

Dealing with Discontentment

Let your conversation be without
covetousness; and be content with
such things as ye have: for he hath
said, I will never leave thee,
nor forsake thee.
Hebrews 13:5 KJV

I have learned in whatever state I am,
to be content: I know how to be
abased, and I know how to abound.
Everywhere and in all things I have
learned both to be full and to be
hungry, both to abound and to suffer
need. I can do all things through
Christ who strengthens me.
Philippians 4:11-13 NKJV

He who dwells in the shelter of the
Most High will rest in the shadow of
the Almighty. I will say of the Lord,
"He is my refuge and my fortress,
my God, in whom I trust."
Psalm 91:1-2

When You Are Discontent

And we know that all things work
together for good to them that love
God, to them who are the called
according to his purpose.
Romans 8:28 KJV

Those who live according to
the sinful nature have their minds
set on what that nature desires;
but those who live in accordance
with the Spirit have their minds
set on what the Spirit desires.
The mind of sinful man is death,
but the mind controlled by
the Spirit is life and peace.
Romans 8:5-6

Not that we are sufficient
of our selves to think any
thing as of ourselves; but
our sufficiency is of God.
2 Corinthians 3:5 KJV

The Truth about Discouragement

Why are you downcast, O my soul?
Why so disturbed within me?
Put your hope in God, for I will yet
praise him, my Savior and my God.
Psalm 43:5

When I remember these things, I
pour out my soul within me. For I
used to go with the multitude; I went
with them to the house of God, with
the voice of joy and praise, with a
multitude that kept a pilgrim feast.
Psalm 42:4 NKJV

Behold, the Lord thy God hath
set the land before thee: go up and
possess it, as the Lord God of
thy fathers hath said unto thee;
fear not, neither be discouraged.
Deuteronomy 1:21 KJV

What To Do about Discouragement

But you, be strong and do not
let your hands be weak, for
your work shall be rewarded!
2 Chronicles 15:7 NKJV

Keep your eyes open for spiritual
danger; stand true to the Lord; act
like men; be strong; and whatever
you do, do it with kindness and love.
1 Corinthians 16:13 TLB

But Christ, God's faithful Son, is in
complete charge of God's house. And
we Christians are God's house—
He lives in us!—if we keep up our
courage firm to the end, and our
joy and our trust in the Lord.
Hebrews 3:6 TLB

How To Be Confident Instead

Being confident of this very thing,
that he which hath begun a good
work in you will perform it
until the day of Jesus Christ.
Philippians 1:6 KJV

Such confidence as this is ours
through Christ before God. Not that
we are competent in ourselves to
claim anything for ourselves, but
our competence comes from God.
2 Corinthians 3:4-5

And we have confidence in the Lord
concerning you, both that you do and
will do the things we command you.
2 Thessalonians 3:4 NKJV

And so, dear brothers, now we
may walk right into the very
Holy of Holies where God is,
because of the blood of Jesus.
Hebrews 10:19 TLB

The Truth about Encouragement

In the day when I cried thou
answeredst me, and strengthenedst
me with strength in my soul.
Though I walk in the midst of
trouble, thou wilt revive me.
Psalm 138:3,7 KJV

But from everlasting to everlasting
the Lord's love is with those who
fear him, and his righteousness
with their children's children—with
those who keep his covenant and
remember to obey his precepts.
Psalm 103:17-18

Be strong and of good courage,
do not fear nor be afraid of them;
for the Lord your God, He is the
One who goes with you. He will
not leave you nor forsake you.
Deuteronomy 31:6 NKJV

How To Receive Encouragement

Be strong and of a good courage; be
not afraid, neither be thou dismayed:
for the Lord thy God is with thee
whithersoever thou goest.
Joshua 1:9 KJV

Trust in the Lord instead. Be kind and
good to others; then you will live
safely here in the land and prosper,
feeding in safety. Be delighted with
the Lord. Then he will give you
all your heart's desires.
Psalm 37:3-4 TLB

The humble shall see their
God at work for them . . .
All who seek for God shall live in joy.
Psalm 69:32 TLB

I can do all things in him
who strengthens me.
Philippians 4:13 RSV

53

God's Little Book of Promises

Encouraging Others

But exhort one another daily,
while it is called "Today," lest any of
you be hardened through the
deceitfulness of sin.
Hebrews 3:13 NKJV

Now go out and
encourage your men.
2 Samuel 19:7

Judas and Silas, who themselves were
prophets, said much to encourage
and strengthen the brothers.
Acts 15:32

Preach the word, be urgent in
season and out of season, convince
rebuke, and exhort, be unfailing
in patience and in teaching.
2 Timothy 4:2 RSV

God's Little Book of Promises

The Truth about Failure

If the Lord delights in a man's way,
he makes his steps firm; though
he stumble, he will not fall, for the
Lord upholds him with his hand.
Psalm 37:23-24

For whatever is born of God
overcomes the world. And this is
the victory that has overcome
the world—our faith.
1 John 5:4 NKJV

Without counsel plans go wrong,
but with many advisers they succeed.
Proverbs 15:22 RSV

The steadfast love of the Lord never
ceases, his mercies never come to an
end; they are new every morning;
great is thy faithfulness.
Lamentations 3:22-23 RSV

What To Do When You Have Failed

With God's help we shall do
mighty things, for he will
trample down our foes.
Psalm 60:12 TLB

If God is for us, who can be against
us? He who did not spare his own
Son, but gave him up for us all—
how will he not also, along with
him, graciously give us all things?
Romans 8:31-32

Now thanks be to God who always
leads us in triumph in Christ, and
through us diffuses the fragrance
of His knowledge in every place.
2 Corinthians 2:14 NKJV

God's Little Book of Promises

God's Promise on Failure

Lift up your eyes to the heavens,
and look upon the earth beneath:
for the heavens shall vanish away
like smoke, and the earth shall
wax old like a garment, and they
that dwell therein shall die in
like manner: but my salvation shall
be for ever, and my righteousness
shall not be abolished.
Isaiah 51:6 KJV

All have sinned and fall short of
the glory of God, being justified freely
by His grace through the redemption
that is in Christ Jesus.
Romans 3:23-24 NKJV

For a just man falleth seven times,
and riseth up again: but the wicked
shall fall into mischief.
Proverbs 24:16 KJV

The Truth about Faith

What is faith? It is the confident
assurance that something we want
is going to happen. It is the certainty
that what we hope for is waiting
for us, even though we cannot
see it up ahead.
Hebrews 11:1 TLB

So now, since we have been made
right in God's sight by faith in his
promises, we can have real peace
with him because of what Jesus
Christ our Lord has done for us. For
because of our faith, he has brought
us into this place of highest privilege
where we now stand, and we
confidently and joyfully look forward
to actually becoming all that God has
had in mind for us to be.
Romans 5:1-2 TLB

For ye are all the children of God
by faith in Christ Jesus.
Galatians 3:26 KJV

What To Do with Faith

Above all, taking the shield of faith,
wherewith ye shall be able to quench
all the fiery darts of the wicked.
Ephesians 6:16 KJV

We live by faith, not by sight.
2 Corinthians 5:7

If you can believe, all things are
possible to him who believes.
Mark 9:23 NKJV

God's Little Book of Promises

God's Faithfulness

And now just as you trusted Christ
to save you, trust him, too,
for each day's problems;
live in vital union with him.
Colossians 2:6 TLB

Whither shall I go from thy spirit?
or whither shall I flee from thy
presence? If I ascend up into heaven,
thou art there: if I make my bed in
hell, behold, thou art there. If I take
the wings of the morning, and dwell
in the uttermost parts of the sea;
Even there shall thy hand lead me,
and thy right hand shall hold me.
Psalm 139:7-10 KJV

My presence shall go with thee,
and I will give thee rest.
Exodus 33:14 KJV

The Truth about Family

A man must leave his father and
mother when he marries, so that he
can be perfectly joined to his wife,
and the two shall be one.
Ephesians 5:31 TLB

Children, obey your parents in the
Lord, for this is right. Honor your
father and mother (which is the first
commandment with a promise), that
it may be well with you, and that
you may live long on the earth.
Ephesians 6:1-3 NASB

Be very careful never to forget what
you have seen God doing for you.
May his miracles have a deep and
permanent effect upon your lives! Tell
your children and your grandchildren
about the glorious miracles he did.
Deuteronomy 4:9 TLB

Treatment of Family

Do not speak evil of one
another, brethren.
James 4:11 NKJV

If anyone says, "I love God," yet
hates his brother, he is a liar. For
anyone who does not love his
brother, whom he has seen, cannot
love God, whom he has not seen.
And he has given us this command:
Whoever loves God must
also love his brother.
1 John 4:20-21

But if anyone does not provide
for his own, and especially
for those of his household,
he has denied the faith,
and is worse than an unbeliever.
1 Timothy 5:8 NASB

God's Little Book of Promises

God's Family

Honor all men; love the brotherhood,
fear God, honor the king.
1 Peter 2:17 NASB

Behold, how good and how
pleasant it is for brothers to
dwell together in unity!
Psalm 133:1 NASB

Truly I say to you, to the extent
that you did it to one of these
brothers of Mine, even the least
of them, you did it to Me.
Matthew 25:40 NASB

Both the one who makes men holy
and those who are made holy are of
the same family. So Jesus is not
ashamed to call them brothers.
Hebrews 2:11

The Truth about Favor

For surely, O Lord, you bless
the righteous; you surround them
with your favor as with a shield.
Psalm 5:12

A good name is to be chosen
rather than great riches, loving favor
rather than silver and gold.
Proverbs 22:1 NKJV

They did not conquer by their own
strength and skill, but by your
mighty power and because you
smiled upon them and favored them.
Psalm 44:3 TLB

For whoever finds me finds life
and wins approval from the Lord.
Proverbs 8:35 TLB

Finding Favor

Never forget to be truthful and kind.
Hold these virtues tightly. Write
them deep within your heart. If you
want favor with both God and man,
and a reputation for good judgment
and common sense, then trust the
Lord completely; don't ever trust
yourself. In everything you do,
put God first, and he will direct you
and crown your efforts with success.
Proverbs 3:3-6 TLB

The Lord sets prisoners free, the
Lord gives sight to the blind, the Lord
lifts up those who are bowed down,
the Lord loves the righteous.
Psalm 146:7-8

God's Favor

And Jesus grew in wisdom
and stature, and in favor
with God and men.
Luke 2:52

In his distress he sought the favor
of the Lord his God and humbled
himself greatly before the
God of his fathers.
2 Chronicles 33:12

But God was with him and
delivered him out of all his troubles,
and gave him favor and wisdom in
the presence of Pharaoh, king of
Egypt; and he made him governor
over Egypt and all his house.
Acts 7:9-10 NKJV

The Truth about Fear

Fear thou not; for I am with thee:
be not dismayed; for I am thy God;
I will strengthen thee; yea, I will
help thee; yea, I will uphold thee with
the right hand of my righteousness.
Isaiah 41:10 KJV

For God did not give us a spirit
of timidity, but a spirit of power,
of love and of self-discipline.
2 Timothy 1:7

Peace I leave with you; my peace I
give you. I do not give to you as the
world gives. Do not let your hearts
be troubled and do not be afraid.
John 14:27

But Jesus ignored their comments and
said . . . "Don't be afraid.
Just trust me."
Mark 5:36 TLB

What To Do about Fear

Be anxious for nothing, but in
everything by prayer and
supplication, with thanksgiving,
let your requests be made known
to God; and the peace of God,
which surpasses all understanding,
will guard your hearts and
minds through Christ Jesus.
Philippians 4:6-7 NKJV

But when I am afraid, I will put
my confidence in you. Yes, I will
trust the promises of God. And
since I am trusting him, what
can mere man do to me?
Psalm 56:3-4 TLB

Be not afraid of sudden fear,
neither of the desolation of the
wicked, when it cometh. For the
Lord shall be thy confidence, and
shall keep thy foot from being taken.
Proverbs 3:25-26 KJV

Confidence in the Midst of Fear

When you go through deep waters
and great trouble, I will be with you.
When you go through rivers of
difficulty, you will not drown! When
you walk through the fire of
oppression, you will not be burned
up—the flames will not consume you.
Isaiah 43:2 TLB

Even though I walk through the
valley of the shadow of death, I will
fear no evil, for you are with me; your
rod and your staff, they comfort me.
Psalm 23:4

The Lord is my light and my
salvation; Whom shall I fear?
The Lord is the strength of my life;
of whom shall I be afraid? When
the wicked came against me to eat up
my flesh, my enemies and my foes,
they stumbled and fell.
Psalm 27:1-2 NKJV

The Truth about Finances

And God is able to make all
grace abound toward you, that you,
always having all sufficiency in all
things, may have an abundance
for every good work.
2 Corinthians 9:8 NKJV

So we should be well satisfied
without money if we have
enough food and clothing.
1 Timothy 6:8 TLB

"Bring the whole tithe into
the storehouse, that there may be
food in my house. Test me in this,"
says the Lord God Almighty, "and
see if I will not throw open the
floodgates of heaven and pour out
so much blessing that you will
not have room enough for it."
Malachi 3:10

When You Are Worried about Finances

I know what it is to be in need,
and I know what it is to have plenty.
I have learned the secret of being
content in any and every situation,
whether well fed or hungry, whether
living in plenty or in want.
Philippians 4:12

Therefore I say to you, do not worry
about your life . . . Look at the birds
of the air, for they neither sow nor
reap nor gather into barns; yet your
heaveny Father feeds them. Are you
not of more value than they?
Matthew 6:25-26 NKJV

God's Riches

Do not lay up for yourselves treasures
on earth, where moth and rust destroy
and where thieves break in and steal;
but lay up for yourselves treasures in
heaven, where neither moth nor rust
destroys and where thieves do not
break in and steal. For where your
treasure is, there your heart will be also.
Matthew 6:19-21 NKJV

And it is he who will supply
all your needs from his riches
in glory, because of what
Christ Jesus has done for us.
Philippians 4:19 TLB

For you know the grace of our
Lord Jesus Christ, that though
He was rich, yet for your sake He
became poor, that you through
His poverty might become rich.
2 Corinthians 8:9 NASB

72

God's Little Book of Promises

The Truth about Forgiveness

If we confess our sins, He is faithful
and just to forgive us our sins and to
cleanse us from all unrighteousness.
1 John 1:9 NKJV

In him we have redemption through
his blood, the forgiveness of our
trespasses, according to the riches of
his grace which he lavished upon us.
Ephesians 1:7-8 RSV

As far as the east is from the west,
so far has he removed our
transgressions from us.
Psalm 103:12

You were dead in sins, and
your sinful desires were not yet
cut away. Then he gave you a
share in the very life of Christ,
for he forgave all your sins.
Colossians 2:13 TLB

How To Receive Forgiveness

If My people who are called by My
name will humble themselves, and
pray and seek My face, and turn
from their wicked ways, then I will
hear from heaven, and will forgive
their sin and heal their land.
2 Chronicles 7:14 NKJV

Then I acknowledged my sin to you
and did not cover up my iniquity.
I said, "I will confess my
transgressions to the Lord"—and
you forgave the guilt of my sin.
Psalm 32:5

Your heavenly Father will forgive
you if you forgive those
who sin against you.
Matthew 6:14 TLB

Giving Forgiveness

But I say: Love your enemies!
Pray for those who persecute you!
In that way you will be acting as
true sons of your Father in heaven.
For he gives his sunlight to both the
evil and the good, and sends rain on
the just and on the unjust too.
Matthew 5:44-45 TLB

And whenever you stand praying,
forgive, if you have anything against
anyone; so that your Father also
who is in heaven may forgive
you your transgressions.
Mark 11:25 NASB

But love your enemies, do good,
and lend, hoping for nothing in
return . . . Therefore be merciful,
just as your Father also is merciful.
Luke 6:35-36 NKJV

The Truth about Giving

Remember this: Whoever sows
sparingly will also reap sparingly,
and whoever sows generously
will also reap generously.
2 Corinthians 9:6

In all things I have shown you that
by so toiling one must help the
weak, remembering the words of the
Lord Jesus, how he said, "It is more
blessed to give than to receive."
Acts 20:35 RSV

Whoever can be trusted with
very little can also be trusted
with much, and whoever is
dishonest with very little will also be
dishonest with much. So if you have
not been trustworthy in handling
worldly wealth, who will trust
you with true riches?
Luke 16:10-11

How To Give

Take heed that you do not do
your charitable deeds before men,
to be seen by them.
Matthew 6:1 NKJV

On every Lord's Day each of you
should put aside something from
what you have earned during the
week, and use if for this offering.
The amount depends on how much
the Lord has helped you earn.
1 Corinthians 16:2 TLB

Give, and it will be given to you.
A good measure, pressed down,
shaken together and running over,
will be poured into your lap.
For the measure you use,
it will be measured to you.
Luke 6:38

Offerings

From what you have, take an
offering for the Lord. Everyone who
is willing is to bring to the Lord an
offering of gold, silver and bronze.
Exodus 35:5

As soon as the commandment
was circulated, the children of Israel
brought in abundance the firstfruits
of grain and wine, oil and honey,
and of all the produce of the field;
and they brought in abundantly
the tithe of everything.
2 Chronicles 31:5 NKJV

Every man shall give as he is able,
according to the blessing of the Lord
your God which he has given you.
Deuteronomy 16:17 RSV

The Truth about Guidance

For this God is our God for ever
and ever; he will be our
guide even to the end.
Psalm 48:14

A man's heart deviseth his way:
but the Lord directeth his steps.
Proverbs 16:9 KJV

The steps of a good man are
ordered by the Lord; and
he delighteth in his way.
Psalm 37:23 KJV

I will instruct you (says the Lord)
and guide you along the best
pathway for your life; I will advise
you and watch your progress.
Psalm 32:8 TLB

The Guidance of God

Then he led forth his people
like sheep, and guided them
in the wilderness like a flock.
Psalm 78:52 RSV

For all who are led by the
Spirit of God are sons of God.
Romans 8:14 RSV

O Lord, you are my light!
You make my darkness bright.
2 Samuel 22:29 TLB

He makes me lie down in green
pastures, he leads me beside quiet
waters, he restores my soul.
He guides me in paths of
righteousness for his name's sake.
Psalm 23:2-3

When You Need Guidance

And the Lord will guide you
continually, and satisfy your desire
with good things, and make your
bones strong; and you shall be
like a watered garden, like a spring
of water, whose waters fail not.
Isaiah 58:11 RSV

When the Holy Spirit, who is truth,
comes, he shall guide you into all
truth, for he will not be presenting
his own ideas, but will be passing
on to you what he has heard.
He will tell you about the future.
John 16:13 TLB

Call unto me, and I will answer thee,
and shew thee great and mighty
things, which thou knowest not.
Jeremiah 33:3 KJV

The Truth about Happiness

For to the man who pleases him
God gives wisdom and
knowledge and joy.
Ecclesiastes 2:26 RSV

A glad heart makes a cheerful
countenance, but by sorrow of
heart the spirit is broken.
Proverbs 15:13 RSV

Happiness or sadness or wealth
should not keep anyone from
doing God's work.
1 Corinthians 7:30 TLB

Happy is the man that
findeth wisdom, and the man
that getteth understanding.
Proverbs 3:13 KJV

When To Be Happy

Is any one among you suffering?
Let him pray. Is any cheerful?
Let him sing praise.
James 5:13 RSV

And those who have reason
to be thankful should continually
be singing praises to the Lord.
James 5:13 TLB

I will bless the Lord at all times;
His praise shall continually
be in my mouth.
Psalm 34:1 NKJV

Showing Happiness

Rejoice in the Lord always.
I will say it again: Rejoice!
Philippians 4:4

For God is the King of all the earth;
sing to him a psalm of praise.
Psalm 47:7

I will praise you with music,
telling of your faithfulness to all
your promises, O Holy One of Israel.
I will shout and sing your praises
for redeeming me. I will talk to
others all day long about your
justice and your goodness.
Psalm 71:22-24 TLB

God's Little Book of Promises

The Truth about Health and Healing

Yes, I will bless the Lord and not
forget the glorious things
he does for me. He forgives all
my sins. He heals me.
Psalm 103:2-3 TLB

Surely He has borne our griefs and
carried our sorrows; yet we esteemed
Him stricken, smitten by God, and
afflicted. But He was wounded for
our transgressions, He was bruised
for our iniquities; the chastisement
for our peace was upon Him, and
by His stripes we are healed.
Isaiah 53:4-5 NKJV

Jesus and Healing

And all the crowd sought to touch
him, for power came forth from him
and healed them all.
Luke 6:19 RSV

Jesus went throughout Galilee,
teaching in their synagogues,
preaching the good news of the
kingdom, and healing every disease
and sickness among the people.
Matthew 4:23

Look! A leper is approaching. He
kneels before him worshiping. "Sir,"
the leper pleads, "if you want to, you
can heal me." Jesus touches the man.
"I want to," he says; "be healed."
And instantly the leprosy disappears.
Matthew 8:2-3 TLB

Believers and Healing

Is anyone among you sick? Let him
call for the elders of the church, and
let them pray over him, anointing him
with oil in the name of the Lord. And
the prayer of faith will save the sick,
and the Lord will raise him up.
And if he has committed sins,
he will be forgiven.
James 5:14-15 NKJV

Heal the sick, raise the dead,
cleanse lepers, cast out demons.
Matthew 10:8 RSV

Little children, you are of God,
and have overcome them;
for he who is in you is greater
than he who is in the world.
1 John 4:4 RSV

The Truth about Hope

Behold, the eye of the Lord is upon
them that fear him, upon them
that hope in his mercy.
Psalm 33:18 KJV

It is good that a man should both
hope and quietly wait for the
salvation of the Lord.
Lamentations 3:26 KJV

Happy is he whose help is the God
of Jacob, whose hope is in the Lord
his God, who made heaven and
earth, the sea, and all that is in them;
who keeps faith for ever.
Psalm 146:5 RSV

Through him we have obtained
access to this grace in which we
stand, and we rejoice in our hope
of sharing the glory of God.
Romans 5:2 RSV

Where To Find Hope

Praise be to the God and Father of
our Lord Jesus Christ! In his great
mercy he has given us new birth
into a living hope through the
resurrection of Jesus Christ from
the dead, and into an inheritance that
can never perish, spoil or fade—kept
in heaven for you.
1 Peter 1:3-4

O Lord, you alone are my hope;
I've trusted you from childhood.
Psalm 71:5 TLB

May those who fear you rejoice
when they see me, for I have
put my hope in your word.
Psalm 119:74

What To Do When You Need Hope

But O my soul, don't be discouraged.
Don't be upset. Expect God to act!
For I know that I shall again have
plenty of reason to praise him for
all that he will do. He is my help!
He is my God!
Psalm 42:11 TLB

Be of good courage, and he
shall strengthen your heart,
all ye that hope in the Lord.
Psalm 31:24 KJV

Put your hope in God, for I will yet
praise him, my Savior and my God.
Psalm 42:5

But let us who are of the day be
sober, putting on the breastplate of
faith and love, and as a helmet
the hope of salvation.
1 Thessalonians 5:8 NKJV

The Truth about Injustice

Happy are those who are persecuted
because they are good, for the
Kingdom of Heaven is theirs. When
you are reviled and persecuted and
lied about because you are my
followers—wonderful! Be happy
about it! Be very glad! for a
tremendous reward awaits you up in
heaven. And remember, the ancient
prophets were persecuted too.
Matthew 5:10-12 TLB

Many are the afflictions of
the righteous: but the Lord
delivereth him out of them all.
Psalm 34:19 KJV

Do not be surprised, my brothers,
if the world hates you.
1 John 3:13

God's Justice

He is the Rock, his work is perfect:
for all his ways are judgment:
a God of truth and without
iniquity, just and right is he.
Deuteronomy 32:4 KJV

Yet ye say, The way of the Lord
is not equal. Hear now, O house
of Israel; is not my way equal?
are not your ways unequal?
Ezekiel 18:25 KJV

Great in counsel and mighty
in deed; whose eyes are open to
all the ways of men, rewarding every
man according to his ways and
according to the fruit of his doings.
Jeremiah 32:19 RSV

Bearing Injustice - A Call To Action

Defend the poor and fatherless;
do justice to the afflicted and needy.
deliver the poor and needy; free them
from the hand of the wicked.
Psalm 82:3-4 NKJV

A generous man will himself
be blessed, for he shares
his food with the poor.
Proverbs 22:9

She opens her arms to the poor
and extends her hands to the needy.
Proverbs 31:20

He has shown you, O man,
what is good; and what does
the Lord require of you but to
do justly, to love mercy, and to
walk humbly with your God?
Micah 6:8 NKJV

The Truth about Integrity

I know, my God, that you test men
to see if they are good; for you
enjoy good men. I have done
all this with good motives, and I
have watched your people offer
their gifts willingly and joyously.
1 Chronicles 29:17 TLB

May integrity and uprightness
preserve me, for I wait for thee.
Psalm 25:21 RSV

He who walks in integrity
walks securely, but he who
perverts his ways will be found out.
Proverbs 10:9 RSV

The integrity of the upright guides
them, but the crookedness of the
treacherous destroys them.
Proverbs 11:3 RSV

How To Maintain Integrity

Till I die, I will not deny my integrity.
Job 27:5

And as for you, if you will walk
before me, as David your father
walked, with integrity of heart and
uprightness, doing according to all
that I have commanded you, and
keeping my statutes and my
ordinances, then I will establish
your royal throne over Israel
for ever, as I promised.
1 Kings 9:4-5 RSV

When the whirlwind passes by, the
wicked is no more, but the righteous
has an everlasting foundation.
Proverbs 10:25 NKJV

By standing firm you will gain life.
Luke 21:19

Biblical Examples of Integrity

By faith Noah, when warned about things not yet seen, in holy fear built an ark to save his family. By his faith he condemned the world and became heir of the righteousness that comes by faith. By faith Abraham, when called to go to a place he would later receive as his inheritance, obeyed and went, even though he did not know where he was going.
Hebrews 11:7-8

And they stoned Stephen as he was calling on God and saying, "Lord Jesus, receive my spirit." Then he knelt down and cried out with a loud voice, "Lord, do not charge them with this sin." And when he had said this, he fell asleep.
Acts 7:59-60 NKJV

The Truth about Jealousy

For where you have envy and
selfish ambition, there you find
disorder and every evil practice.
James 3:16

Be still before the Lord and wait
patiently for him; do not fret when
men succeed in their ways, when
they carry out their wicked schemes.
Psalm 37:7

If we live by the Spirit, let us also
walk by the Spirit. Let us have no
self-conceit, no provoking of one
another, no envy of one another.
Galatians 5:25-26 RSV

You shall not covet your neighbor's
house; you shall not covet your
neighbor's wife, nor his male servant,
nor his female servant, nor his ox,
nor his donkey, nor anything
that is your neighbor's.
Exodus 20:17 NKJV

The Ugliness of Jealousy

For the wicked boasteth of his heart's
desire, and blesseth the covetous,
whom the Lord abhorreth.
Psalm 10:3 KJV

Wrath is cruel, anger is
overwhelming; but who can
stand before jealousy?
Proverbs 27:4 RSV

Then I observed that the basic
motive for success is the driving
force of envy and jealousy! But this,
too, is foolishness, chasing the wind.
Ecclesiastes 4:4 TLB

Do not envy wicked men,
do not desire their company,
for their hearts plot violence, and
their lips talk about making trouble.
Proverbs 24:1-2

But if you harbor bitter envy and
selfish ambition in your hearts, do
not boast about it or deny the truth.
James 3:14

Who Can Have Proper Jealousy

Do you think that the Scripture
says in vain, "The Spirit who
dwells in us yearns jealously"?
James 4:5 NKJV

You shall not make for yourself
an idol in the form of anything in
heaven above or on the earth
beneath or in the waters below.
You shall not bow down to them or
worship them; for I, the Lord
your God, am a jealous God.
Exodus 20:4-5

Be careful not to forget the covenant
of the Lord your God that he made
with you; do not make for yourselves
an idol in the form of anything the
Lord your God has forbidden.
For the Lord your God is a
consuming fire, a jealous God.
Deuteronomy 4:23-24

The Truth about Joy

For you shall go out in joy and be
led forth in peace; the mountains and
the hills before you shall break forth
into singing, and all the trees of the
field shall clap their hands.
Isaiah 55:12 RSV

And the ransomed of the Lord shall
return, and come to Zion with
singing; everlasting joy shall be
upon their heads; they shall obtain
joy and gladness, and sorrow and
sighing shall flee away.
Isaiah 51:11 RSV

Then he said to them, "Go your way,
eat the fat and drink sweet wine and
send portions to him for whom
nothing is prepared; for this day
is holy to our Lord; and do not
be grieved, for the joy of the
Lord is your strength."
Nehemiah 8:10 RSV

Joy in God

No wonder we are happy in the Lord!
For we are trusting him.
We trust his holy name.
Psalm 33:21 TLB

I will greatly rejoice in the Lord,
my soul shall exult in my God;
for he has clothed me with the
garments of salvation, he has
covered me with the robe of
righteousness, as the bridegroom
decks himself with the garland,
and as a bride adorns
herself with her jewels.
Isaiah 61:10 RSV

My soul is feasted as with marrow
and fat, and my mouth praises thee
with joyful lips, when I think of thee
upon my bed, and meditate on thee
in the watches of the night.
Psalm 63:5-6 RSV

Joyful People

Yes, the gladness you have given
me is far greater than their joys
at harvest time as they gaze
at their bountiful crops.
Psalm 4:7 TLB

May those who sow in tears reap
with shouts of joy! He that goes
forth weeping, bearing the seed
for sowing, shall come home
with shouts of joy, bringing
his sheaves with him.
Psalm 126:5-6 RSV

So you have sorrow now,
but I will see you again and
your hearts will rejoice, and no one
will take your joy from you.
John 16:22 RSV

God's Little Book of Promises

The Truth about Justice

As for the Almighty, we cannot find
Him; He is excellent in power,
in judgment and abundant justice;
He does not oppress.
Job 37:23 NKJV

Arise, O Lord, in thy anger, lift thyself
up against the fury of my enemies;
awake, O my God, thou hast
appointed a judgment.
Psalm 7:6 RSV

But let him who glories glory in this,
that he understands and knows me,
that I am the Lord who practice
steadfast love, justice, and
righteousness in the earth;
for in these things I delight.
Jeremiah 9:24 RSV

God's Justice

He does not crush the weak,
or quench the smallest hope;
he will end all conflict with his final
victory, and his name shall be
the hope of all the world.
Matthew 12:20-21 TLB

God presented him as a sacrifice
of atonement, through faith in his
blood. He did this to demonstrate
his justice, because in his forbearance
he had left the sins committed
beforehand unpunished.
Romans 3:25

The Lord has made himself known,
he has executed judgment,
the wicked are snared in
the work of their own hands.
Psalm 9:16 RSV

Finding Justice

Follow justice and justice alone,
so that you may live and
possess the land the Lord
your God is giving you.
Deuteronomy 16:20

The king's strength also loveth
judgment; thou dost establish equity,
thou executest judgment and
righteousness in Jacob.
Psalm 99:4 KJV

Learn to do well; seek judgment,
relieve the oppressed, judge the
fatherless, plead for the widow.
Isaiah 1:17 KJV

But let justice roll down like waters,
and righteousness like
an everflowing stream.
Amos 5:24 RSV

The Truth about Loneliness

Behold, I am with you and will keep
you wherever you go, and will bring
you back to this land; for I will not
leave you until I have done that of
which I have spoken to you.
Genesis 28:15 RSV

God sets the lonely in families,
he leads forth the prisoners
with singing.
Psalm 68:6

All those who know your mercy,
Lord, will count on you for help.
For you have never yet forsaken
those who trust in you.
Psalm 9:10 TLB

I will never, never fail you
nor forsake you.
Hebrews 13:5 TLB

What To Do When You Are Lonely

The eternal God is thy refuge, and underneath are the everlasting arms.
Deuteronomy 33:27 KJV

Who shall separate us from the love of Christ? Shall tribulation, or distress, or perscution, or famine, or nakedness, or peril, or sword? Yet in all these things we are more than conquerors through Him who loved us. For I am persuaded that neither death nor life, nor angels nor principalities nor powers, nor things present nor things to come, nor height nor depth, nor any other created thing, shall be able to separate us from the love of God which is in Christ Jesus our Lord.
Romans 8:35,37-39 NKJV

Solitude Instead of Loneliness

Be still, and know that I am God;
I will be exalted among the nations,
I will be exalted in the earth.
Psalm 46:10

We have thought, O God,
on Your lovingkindness,
in the midst of Your temple.
Psalm 48:9 NKJV

Early in the morning, before the sun
is up, I am praying and pointing
out how much I trust in you.
I stay awake through the night
to think about your promises.
Psalm 119:147-148 TLB

You are my hiding place from every
storm of life; you even keep me from
getting into trouble! You surround
me with songs of victory.
Psalm 32:7 TLB

The Truth about Loss

"And God will wipe away every tear
from their eyes; there shall be no
more death, nor sorrow, nor crying.
There shall be no more pain, for the
former things have passed away."
Then He who sat on the throne said,
"Behold, I make all things new."
Revelation 21:4-5 NKJV

Weeping may remain for a night,
but rejoicing comes in the morning.
Psalm 30:5

He heals the brokenhearted
and binds up their wounds.
Psalm 147:3 NKJV

There is a time for everything,
and a season for every activity
under heaven . . . a time to mourn
and a time to dance.
Ecclesiastes 3:1,4

Strength for Loss

To all who mourn in Israel he will
give: Beauty for ashes; Joy instead
of mourning; Praise instead of
heaviness. For God has planted
them like strong and graceful
oaks for his own glory.
Isaiah 61:3 TLB

Blessed are those who mourn,
for they will be comforted.
Matthew 5:4

Shout for joy, O heavens; rejoice,
O earth; burst into song,
O mountains! For the Lord
comforts his people and will have
compassion on his afflicted ones.
Isaiah 49:13

For as the sufferings of Christ
abound in us, so our consolation
also abounds through Christ.
2 Corinthians 1:5 NKJV

Comforting Those with Loss

Rejoice with those who rejoice;
mourn with those who mourn.
Romans 12:15

I will turn their mourning into
gladness; I will give them comfort
and joy instead of sorrow.
Jeremiah 31:13

Therefore, as the elect of God,
holy and beloved, put on tender
mercies, kindness, humility,
meekness, longsuffering.
Colossians 3:12 NKJV

Blessed be the God and Father of
our Lord Jesus Christ, the Father of
mercies and God of all comfort, who
comforts us in all our tribulation, that
we may be able to comfort those who
are in any trouble, with the comfort
with which we ourselves are
comforted by God.
2 Corinthians 1:3-4 NKJV

The Truth about Love

And now these three remain: faith, hope and love. But the greatest of these is love.
1 Corinthians 13:13

Work instead at what is right and good, learning to trust him and love others, and to be patient and gentle.
1 Timothy 6:11 TLB

And above all things have fervent love for one another, for "love will cover a multitude of sins."
1 Peter 4:8 NKJV

And above all these put on love, which binds everything together in perfect harmony.
Colossians 3:14 RSV

God's Little Book of Promises

Love Between God and Man

For God so loved the world that
he gave his only Son, that whoever
believes in him should not perish
but have eternal life.
John 3:16 RSV

And he will love thee,
and bless thee, and multiply thee.
Deuteronomy 7:13 KJV

The Lord sets prisoners free, the Lord
gives sight to the blind, the Lord lifts
up those who are bowed down,
the Lord loves the righteous.
Psalm 146:7-8

The Lord your God is with you,
he is mighty to save. He will take
great delight in you, he will
quiet you with his love, he will rejoice
over you with singing.
Zephaniah 3:17

Love between People

You shall not take vengeance, nor
bear any grudge against the children
of your people, but you shall love
your neighbor as yourself:
I am the Lord.
Leviticus 19:18 NKJV

For the whole Law can be
summed up in this one command:
"Love others as you love yourself."
Galatians 5:14 TLB

By this all men will know that
you are my disciples, if you
have love for one another.
John 13:35 RSV

Beloved, let us love one another;
for love is of God, and he who loves
is born of God and knows God.
He who does not love does not
know God; for God is love.
1 John 4:7-8 RSV

The Truth about Marriage

And the Lord God said, It is not good
that the man should be alone; I will
make him an help meet for him.
Genesis 2:18 KJV

Therefore what God has joined
together, let man not separate.
Matthew 19:6

He who finds a wife finds
a good thing, and obtains
favor from the Lord.
Proverbs 18:22 NKJV

Marriage should be honored by all,
and the marriage bed kept pure,
for God will judge the adulterer
and all the sexually immoral.
Hebrews 13:4

Husband and Wife

Therefore a man leaves his father and
his mother and cleaves to his wife,
and they become one flesh.
Genesis 2:24 RSV

You wives, submit yourselves to
your husbands, for that is what
the Lord has planned for you. And
you husbands must be loving and
kind to your wives and not bitter
against them, nor harsh.
Colossians 3:18-19 TLB

You husbands must be careful of
your wives, being thoughtful of their
needs and honoring them . . .
Remember that you and your wife
are partners in receiving
God's blessings.
1 Peter 3:7 TLB

Some Marriage Guidelines

Wives, fit in with your husbands'
plans; for then if they refuse to listen
when you talk to them about the
Lord, they will be won by your
respectful, pure behavior.
1 Peter 3:1 TLB

For the wife does not rule over her
own body, but the husband does;
likewise the husband does not rule
over his own body, but the wife does.
1 Corinthians 7:4 RSV

The unbelieving husband is
consecrated through his wife, and
the unbelieving wife is consecrated
through her husband.
1 Corinthians 7:14 RSV

The Truth about Mercy

Let us therefore come boldly unto
the throne of grace, that we may
obtain mercy, and find grace
to help in time of need.
Hebrews 4:16 KJV

I will make all my goodness pass
before thee, and I will proclaim the
name of the Lord before thee; and
will be gracious to whom I will be
gracious, and will shew mercy on
whom I will shew mercy.
Exodus 33:19 KJV

Give knowledge of salvation to
his people in the forgiveness
of their sins, through the
tender mercy of our God.
Luke 1:77-78 RSV

God's Little Book of Promises

God's Mercy

The Lord is gracious, and full of
compassion; slow to anger,
and of great mercy. The Lord
is good to all: and his tender
mercies are over all his works.
Psalm 145:8-9 KJV

Who is a God like you, who pardons
sin and forgives the transgression
of the remnant of his inheritance? You
do not stay angry forever
but delight to show mercy.
Micah 7:18

Foreigners will come and build
your cities. Presidents and kings will
send you aid. For though I destroyed
you in my anger, I will have mercy on
you through my grace.
Isaiah 60:10 TLB

Finding Mercy

For thou, Lord, art good, and ready
to forgive; and plenteous in mercy
unto all them that call upon thee.
Psalm 86:5 KJV

Yet the Lord still waits for you to
come to him, so he can show you
his love; he will conquer you to
bless you, just as he said. For the
Lord is faithful to his promises.
Blessed are all those who wait
for him to help them.
Isaiah 30:18 TLB

But the lovingkindness of the Lord
is from everlasting to everlasting,
to those who reverence him; his
salvation is to children's children
of those who are faithful to his
covenant and remember to obey him!
Psalm 103:17-18 TLB

The Truth about Obedience

And Samuel said, Hath the Lord
as great delight in burnt offerings
and sacrifices, as in obeying
the voice of the Lord? Behold to obey
is better than sacrifice, and to
hearken than the fat of rams.
1 Samuel 15:22 KJV

Therefore, O Israel, listen closely to
each command and be careful to obey
it, so that all will go well with you,
and so that you will have many
children. If you obey these commands
you will become a great nation in a
glorious land "flowing with milk and
honey," even as the God of your
fathers promised you.
Deuteronomy 6:3 TLB

If they obey and serve him,
they will spend the rest of their
days in prosperity and their
years in contentment.
Job 36:11

Obedient Examples

He who has my commandments and
keeps them, he it is who loves me;
and he who loves me will be loved
by my Father, and I will love him
and manifest myself to him.
John 14:21 RSV

Because of your obedience, the Lord
your God will keep his part of the
contract which, in his tender love,
he made with your fathers.
Deuteronomy 7:12 TLB

When you obey me you are living
in my love, just as I obey
my Father and live in his love.
John 15:10 TLB

It was after he had proved himself
perfect in this experience that Jesus
became the Giver of eternal salvation
to all those who obey him.
Hebrews 5:9 TLB

Being Obedient

And this world is fading away, and these evil, forbidden things will go with it, but whoever keeps doing the will of God will live forever.
1 John 2:17 TLB

And how can we be sure that we belong to him? By looking within ourselves: are we really trying to do what he wants us to?
1 John 2:3 TLB

My son, forget not my law; but let thine heart keep my commandments: For length of days, and long life, and peace, shall they add to thee.
Proverbs 3:1-2 KJV

But, dearly loved friends, if our consciences are clear, we can come to the Lord with perfect assurance and trust, and get whatever we ask for because we are obeying him and doing the things that please him.
1 John 3:21-22 TLB

The Truth about Patience

You need to keep on patiently doing
God's will if you want him to do for
you all that he has promised.
Hebrews 10:36 TLB

Dear brothers, is your life full of
difficulties and temptations? Then be
happy, for when the way is rough,
your patience has a chance to grow.
So let it grow, and don't try to
squirm out of your problems. For
when your patience is finally in full
bloom, then you will be ready for
anything, strong in character,
full and complete.
James 1:2-4 TLB

For ye have need of patience,
that, after ye have done the will of
God, ye might receive the promise.
Hebrews 10:36 KJV

Godly Patience

But You, O Lord, are a God
full of compassion, and gracious,
longsuffering and abundant
in mercy and truth.
Psalm 86:15 NKJV

The Lord is merciful and gracious,
slow to anger, and plenteous in mercy.
He will not always chide: neither will
he keep his anger for ever.
Psalm 103:8-9 KJV

And he passed in front of Moses,
proclaiming, "The Lord, the Lord,
the compassionate and gracious God,
slow to anger, abounding in love
and faithfulness, maintaining
love to thousands, and forgiving
wickedness, rebellion and sin."
Exodus 34:6

Brotherly Patience

And so, as those who have been
chosen of God, holy and beloved,
put on a heart of compassion,
kindness, humility, gentleness and
patience; bearing with one another,
and forgiving each other, whoever
has a complaint against anyone;
just as the Lord forgave you,
so also should you.
Colossians 3:12-13 NASB

Be humble and gentle. Be
patient with each other, making
allowance for each other's faults
because of your love.
Ephesians 4:2 TLB

You will be anxious to follow the
example of those who receive all that
God has promised them because
of their strong faith and patience.
Hebrews 6:12 TLB

The Truth about Persecution

Remember the word that I said
to you, "A servant is not greater
than his master." If they persecuted
Me, they will also persecute you.
John 15:20 NKJV

Blessed are those who have
been persecuted for the sake
of righteousness, for theirs is
the kingdom of heaven. Blessed are
you when men cast insults at you,
and persecute you, and say all kinds
of evil against you falsely,
on account of Me.
Matthew 5:10 NASB

Yes, and those who decide to please
Christ Jesus by living godly lives
will suffer at the hands of
those who hate him.
2 Timothy 3:12 TLB

Handling Persecution

But we have this treasure in earthen
vessels, that the surpassing greatness
of the power may be of God and
not from ourselves; we are afflicted
in every way, but not crushed;
perplexed, but not despairing;
persecuted, but not forsaken; struck
down, but not destroyed; always
carrying about in the body the dying
of Jesus, that the life of Jesus also
may be manifested in our body.
2 Corinthians 4:7-11 NASB

Who shall separate us from the love
of Christ? Shall trouble or hardship
or persecution or famine or
nakedness or danger or sword?
No, in all these things we are
more than conquerors through
him who loved us.
Romans 8:35,37

Your Persecutors

I say: Love your enemies!
Pray for those who persecute you!
In that way you will be acting as
true sons of your Father in heaven.
Matthew 5:44 TLB

If someone mistreats you because
you are a Christian, don't curse him;
pray that God will bless him.
Romans 12:14 TLB

If your enemy is hungry, give him
food to eat; and if he is thirsty, give
him water to drink; for you will
heap burning coals on his head,
and the Lord will reward you.
Proverbs 25:21-22 NASB

The Truth about Perseverance

May the Lord direct your hearts into
God's love and Christ's perseverance.
2 Thessalonians 3:5

[Love] always protects, always trusts,
always hopes, always perseveres.
1 Corinthians 13:7

"My grace is sufficient for you,
for my power is made perfect in
weakness." Therefore I will boast
all the more gladly about my
weaknesses, so that Christ's
power may rest on me.
2 Corinthians 12:9

Under Trials

We also glory in tribulations,
knowing that tribulation produces
perseverance; and perseverance,
character; and character, hope.
Now hope does not disappoint,
because the love of God has been
poured out in our hearts by the
Holy Spirit who was given to us.
Romans 5:3-5 NKJV

Because you know that the testing
of your faith develops perseverance.
Perseverance must finish its work
so that you may be mature and
complete, not lacking anything.
James 1:3-4

But if anyone suffers as a Christian,
let him not feel ashamed, but in
that name let him glorify God.
1 Peter 4:16 NASB

Benefits of Perseverance

You need to persevere so that when
you have done the will of God, you
will receive what he has promised.
Hebrews 10:36

Take heed to yourself and to the
doctrine. Continue in them,
for in doing this you will save both
yourself and those who hear you.
1 Timothy 4:16 NKJV

But the seed of good soil stands for
those with a noble and good heart,
who hear the word, retain it, and
by persevering produce a crop.
Luke 8:15

The Truth about Protection

If you make the Most High
your dwelling—even the Lord,
who is my refuge—then no harm will
befall you, no disaster will come near
your tent. For he will command his
angels concerning you to
guard you in all your ways.
Psalm 91:9-11

No weapon forged against you will
prevail, and you will refute every
tongue that accuses you. This is the
heritage of the servants of the Lord,
and this is their vindication from me.
Isaiah 54:17

In peace I will both lie down and
sleep; for thou alone, O Lord,
makest me dwell in safety.
Psalm 4:8 RSV

Divine Protection

Fear not, for I am with you,
be not dismayed, for I am your
God; I will strengthen you, I will
help you, I will uphold you with
my victorious right hand.
Isaiah 41:10 RSV

The Lord shall preserve you from all
evil; He shall preserve your soul.
The Lord shall preserve your going
out and your coming in from this
time forth, and even forevermore.
Psalm 121:7-8 NKJV

When you pass through the waters,
I will be with you; and when
you pass through the rivers,
they will not sweep over you.
When you walk through the fire,
you will not be burned;
the flames will not set you ablaze.
Isaiah 43:2

Finding Protection

The angel of the Lord encamps
around those who fear him,
and he delivers them. Taste and see
that the Lord is good; blessed is the
man who takes refuge in him.
Psalm 34:7-8

The Lord is a strong fortress.
The godly run to him and are safe.
Proverbs 18:10 TLB

He does not fear bad news, nor
live in dread of what may happen.
For he is settled in his mind that
Jehovah will take care of him.
Psalm 112:7 TLB

The Truth about Provision

The Lord is my shepherd,
I shall not want.
Psalm 23:1 RSV

Don't worry about things—food,
drink, and clothes. For you
already have life and a body—
and they are far more important
than what to eat and wear.
Matthew 6:25 TLB

For your Father knoweth
what things ye have need of,
before ye ask him.
Matthew 6:8 KJV

His divine power hath given
unto us all things that pertain
unto life and godliness.
2 Peter 1:3 KJV

God's Provision

But my God shall supply
all your need according to his
riches in glory by Christ Jesus.
Philippians 4:19 KJV

He causes the grass to grow
for the cattle, and vegetation for the
service of man, that he may bring
forth food from the earth.
Psalm 104:14 NKJV

And God is able to make all grace
abound to you, so that in all things
at all times, having all that you need,
you will abound in every good work.
2 Corinthians 9:8

Man's Role

Do not be anxious about anything,
but in everything, by prayer and
petition, with thanksgiving, present
your requests to God. And the peace
of God, which transcends all
understanding, will guard your hearts
and your minds in Christ Jesus.
Philippians 4:6-7

Oh, fear the Lord, you His saints!
There is no want to those
who fear Him.
Psalm 34:9 NKJV

Trust in the Lord instead. Be kind
and good to others; then you will live
safely here in the land and prosper,
feeding in safety. Be delighted with
the Lord. Then he will give you
all your heart's desires. Commit
everything you do to the Lord. Trust
him to help you do it and he will.
Psalm 37:3-5 TLB

God's Little Book of Promises

The Truth about Reconciliation

Pursue peace with all people,
and holiness, without which no one
will see the Lord: looking carefully
lest anyone fall short of the grace of
God; lest any root of bitterness
springing up cause trouble, and
by this many become defiled.
Hebrews 12:14-15 NKJV

Blessed are the merciful:
for they shall obtain mercy.
Matthew 5:7 KJV

Do not be overcome by evil,
but overcome evil with good.
Romans 12:21

Be kind and compassionate
to one another, forgiving each other,
just as in Christ God forgave you.
Ephesians 4:32

When You Are Wronged

The discretion of a man makes
him slow to anger, and his glory is
to overlook a transgression.
Proverbs 19:11 NKJV

Do not resist an evil person.
If someone strikes you on the right
cheek, turn to him the other also.
Matthew 5:39

And whenever you stand praying,
forgive, if you have anything
against any one; so that your
Father also who is in heaven may
forgive you your trespasses.
Mark 11:25 RSV

Take heed to yourselves: If thy
brother trespass against thee, rebuke
him; and if he repent, forgive him.
Luke 17:3 KJV

When You Are Wrong

But love your enemies, and do good,
and lend, expecting nothing in return;
and your reward will be great,
and you will be sons of the
Most High; for he is kind to
the ungrateful and the selfish.
Luke 6:35 RSV

Why do you look at the speck of
sawdust in your brother's eye and
pay no attention to the plank in
your own eye? How can you say
to your brother, "Let me take this
speck out of your eye," when all the
time there is a plank in your own
eye? You hypocrite, first take the
plank out of your own eye, and then
you will see clearly to remove the
speck from your brother's eye.
Matthew 7:3-5

The Truth about Rejection

Behold what manner of love the
Father has bestowed on us, that we
should be called children of God!
Therefore the world does not know
us, because it did not know Him.
Beloved, now we are children
of God; and it has not yet
been revealed what we shall be,
but we know that when He is
revealed, we shall be like Him,
for we shall see Him as He is.
1 John 3:1-2 NKJV

A man of many companions may
come to ruin, but there is a friend
who sticks closer than a brother.
Proverbs 18:24

When You Feel Rejected

For he chose us in him before the creation of the world to be holy and blameless in his sight. In love he predestined us to be adopted as his sons through Jesus Christ, in accordance with his pleasure and will—to the praise of his glorious grace, which he has freely given us in the One he loves.
Ephesians 1:4-6

For the Lord will not forsake his people; he will not abandon his heritage; for justice will return to the righteous, and all the upright in heart will follow it.
Psalm 94:14-15 RSV

Hope for the Rejected

The poor and needy seek water,
but there is none, Their tongues
fail for thirst. I, the Lord,
will hear them; I, the God of
Israel, will not forsake them.
Isaiah 41:17 NKJV

And Jesus said, "Neither do I
condemn you; go your way.
From now on sin no more."
John 8:11 NASB

He was despised and forsaken
of men, a man of sorrows, and
acquainted with grief; and like one
from whom men hide their face,
He was despised, and we
did not esteem Him. Surely
our griefs He Himself bore,
and our sorrows He carried.
Isaiah 53:3-4 NASB

The Truth about Relationships

God, who has called you
into fellowship with his Son
Jesus Christ our Lord, is faithful.
1 Corinthians 1:9

But if we walk in the light, as he is
in the light, we have fellowship with
one another, and the blood of Jesus,
his Son, purifies us from all sin.
1 John 1:7

And the Scripture was fulfilled
which says, "Abraham believed God,
and it was accounted to him for
righteousness." And he was
called the friend of God.
James 2:23 NKJV

My command is this: Love each other
as I have loved you. Greater love has
no one than this, that he lay down his
life for his friends. You are my friends
if you do what I command.
John 15:12-14

Family Relations

Children, obey your parents
in the Lord: for this is right.
Ephesians 6:1 KJV

Only be careful, and watch
yourselves closely so that you do
not forget the things your eyes have
seen or let them slip from your heart
as long as you live. Teach them
to your children and to their
children after them.
Deuteronomy 4:9

Marriage is honorable among all,
and the bed undefiled.
Hebrews 13:4 NKJV

For the wife does not rule over her
own body, but the husband does;
likewise the husband does not rule
over his own body, but the wife does.
1 Corinthians 7:4 RSV

Other Relationships

A friend loves at all times.
Proverbs 17:17

Do not forsake your friend and the
friend of your father.
Proverbs 27:10

Therefore if you bring your gift to
the altar, and there remember that
your brother has something against
you, leave your gift there before
the altar, and go your way. First be
reconciled to your brother, and
then come and offer your gift.
Matthew 5:23-24 NKJV

Keep on loving each
other as brothers.
Hebrews 13:1

The Truth about Renewal

And do not be conformed to this
world, but be transformed by the
renewing of your mind, that you
may prove what is that good and
acceptable and perfect will of God.
Romans 12:2 NKJV

A new heart I will give you, and
a new spirit I will put within you;
and I will take out of your flesh the
heart of stone and give you a heart
of flesh. And I will put my spirit
within you, and cause you to walk
in my statutes and be careful
to observe my ordinances.
Ezekiel 36:26-27 RSV

If we confess our sins, he is faithful
and just to forgive us our sins, and to
cleanse us from all unrighteousness.
1 John 1:9 KJV

God's Renewal

Create in me a clean heart, O God;
and renew a right spirit within me.
Psalm 51:10 KJV

Therefore if any man be in Christ,
he is a new creature: old things
are passed away; behold,
all things are become new.
2 Corinthians 5:17 KJV

I will seek that which was lost,
and bring again that which was
driven away, and will bind up
that which was broken, and will
strengthen that which was sick:
but I will destroy the fat and
the strong; I will feed them
with judgment.
Ezekiel 34:16 KJV

Renewed Believers

Be made new in the attitude of your
minds; and . . . put on the new self,
created to be like God in true
righteousness and holiness.
Ephesians 4:23-24

Brothers, I do not consider myself
yet to have taken hold of it. But one
thing I do: Forgetting what is behind
and straining toward what is ahead,
I press on toward the goal to win
the prize for which God has called
me heavenward in Christ Jesus.
Philippians 3:13-14

Do not lie to one another,
since you have put off the
old man with his deeds, and
have put on the new man who is
renewed in knowledge according to
the image of Him who created him.
Colossians 3:9-10 NKJV

The Truth about Restoration

Restore to me the joy of thy salvation,
and uphold me with a willing spirit.
The sacrifice acceptable to God is a
broken spirit; a broken and contrite
heart, O God, thou wilt not despise.
Psalm 51;12,17 RSV

Restore us, O God;
make your face shine upon us,
that we may be saved.
Psalm 80:3

Turn us back to You, O Lord,
and we will be restored;
Renew our days as of old.
Lamentations 5:21 NKJV

God's Role

The Lord will restore the splendor
of Jacob like the splendor of Israel,
though destroyers have laid them
waste and have ruined their vines.
Nahum 2:2

And the God of all grace, who called
you to his eternal glory in Christ,
after you have suffered a little while,
will himself restore you and make
you strong, firm and steadfast.
To him be the power for ever
and ever. Amen.
1 Peter 5:10-11

He restores my soul.
Psalm 23:3 NKJV

Our Role

Repent, and let every one of you
be baptized in the name of
Jesus Christ for the remission
of sins; and you shall receive
the gift of the Holy Spirit.
Acts 2:38 NKJV

Cast away from you all your
transgressions, whereby ye
have transgressed; and make
you a new heart and a new spirit.
Ezekiel 18:31 KJV

Repent ye therefore, and be
converted, that your sins may be
blotted out, when the times of
refreshing shall come from
the presence of the Lord.
Acts 3:19 KJV

The Truth about Resurrection

Jesus said to her, "I am the
resurrection and the life. He who
believes in Me, though he may die,
he shall live. And whoever lives and
believes in Me shall never die."
John 11:25-26 NKJV

In a moment, in the twinkling
of an eye, at the last trump:
for the trumpet shall sound, and the
dead shall be raised incorruptible,
and we shall be changed.
1 Corinthians 15:52 KJV

You were also raised up with Him
through faith in the working of God,
who raised Him from the dead.
Colossians 2:12 NASB

Christ's Resurrection

Seeing what was ahead, he spoke of
the resurrection of the Christ, that he
was not abandoned to the grave,
nor did his body see decay. God
has raised this Jesus to life, and
we are all witnesses of the fact.
Exalted to the right hand of God,
he has received from the Father the
promised Holy Spirit and has poured
out what you now see and hear.
Acts 2:31-33

Blessed be the God and Father of our
Lord Jesus Christ, who according to
His abundant mercy has begotten us
again to a living hope through the
resurrection of Jesus Christ from the
dead, to an inheritance incorruptible
and undefiled and that does not fade
away, reserved in heaven for you,
who are kept by the power of God
through faith for salvation ready
to be revealed in the last time.
1 Peter 1:3-5 NKJV

Believers' Resurrection

For if we have been united together
in the likeness of His death,
certainly we also shall be in the
likeness of His resurrection.
Romans 6:5 NKJV

As in Adam all die, so in
Christ all will be made alive.
1 Corinthians 15:22 NASB

I want to know Christ and the
power of his resurrection and
the fellowship of sharing in his
sufferings, becoming like him in his
death, and so, somehow, to attain
to the resurrection from the dead.
Philippians 3:10-11

And Jesus said to him,
"Assuredly, I say to you, today
you will be with Me in Paradise."
Luke 23:43 NKJV

The Truth about Shame

Fear not; you will no longer live
in shame. The shame of your youth
and the sorrows of widowhood
will be remembered no more.
Isaiah 54:4 TLB

Indeed, let no one who
waits on You be ashamed;
let those be ashamed who deal
treacherously without cause.
Psalm 25:3 NKJV

May those who hope in you not be
disgraced because of me, O Lord,
the Lord Almighty; may those who
seek you not be put to shame.
Psalm 69:6

Behold, I lay in Zion a stumbling
stone and rock of offense, and
whoever believes on Him
will not be put to shame.
Romans 9:33 NKJV

Hope for Shame

We are able to hold our heads high
no matter what happens and know
that all is well, for we know how
dearly God loves us, and we feel this
warm love everywhere within us
because God has given us the Holy
Spirit to fill our hearts with his love.
Romans 5:5 TLB

Therefore being justified by faith,
we have peace with God
through our Lord Jesus Christ.
Romans 5:1 KJV

There is therefore now no
condemnation for those
who are in Christ Jesus.
Romans 8:1 NASB

God's Little Book of Promises

Not Ashamed

But if anyone suffers as a Christian,
let him not feel ashamed,
but in that name let him glorify God.
1 Peter 4:16 NASB

For I am not ashamed of the
gospel of Christ, for it is the power
of God to salvation for everyone
who believes, for the Jew . . .
and also for the Greek.
Romans 1:16 NKJV

So do not be ashamed to testify
about our Lord, or ashamed
of me his prisoner.
2 Timothy 1:8

Be diligent to present yourself
approved to God, a worker who
does not need to be ashamed,
rightly dividing the word of truth.
2 Timothy 2:15 NKJV

The Truth about Stewardship

He who is faithful in what is
least is faithful also in much;
and he who is unjust in what is
least is unjust also in much.
Luke 16:10 NKJV

Now it is required that those
who have been given a trust
must prove faithful.
1 Corinthians 4:2

As each one has received a gift,
minister it to one another,
as good stewards of the
manifold grace of God.
1 Peter 4:10 NKJV

Good will come to him who is
generous and lends freely, who
conducts his affairs with justice.
Psalm 112:5

Godly Stewards

Moreover it is required in stewards
that one be found faithful.
1 Corinthians 4:2 NKJV

And he sat down opposite the
treasury, and watched the multitude
putting money into the treasury. Many
rich people put in large sums. And a
poor widow came, and put in two
copper coins, which make a penny.
And he called his disciples to him,
and said to them, "Truly, I say to you,
this poor widow has put in more than
all those who are contributing to the
treasury. For they all contributed out
of their abundance; but she out of her
poverty has put in everything
she had, her whole living."
Mark 12:41-44 RSV

How To Be Stewardly

So when you give to the needy,
do not announce it with trumpets, as
the hypocrites do in the synagogues
and on the streets, to be honored by
men. I tell you the truth, they have
received their reward in full. But
when you give to the needy, do not
let your left hand know what your
right hand is doing, so that your
giving may be in secret.
Matthew 6:2-4

Command those who are rich in this
present age not to be haughty, nor to
trust in uncertain riches but in the
living God, who gives us richly all
things to enjoy. Let them do good,
that they be rich in good works,
ready to give, willing to share.
1 Timothy 6:17-18 NKJV

The Truth about Strength

The Lord is my strength and song,
and he is become my salvation:
he is my God, and I will prepare
him an habitation; my father's
God, and I will exalt him.
Exodus 15:2 KJV

He will give his people strength.
He will bless them with peace.
Psalm 29:11 TLB

My grace is sufficient for you, for My
strength is made perfect in weakness.
2 Corinthians 12:9 NKJV

Finally, my brethren, be strong in the
Lord, and in the power of his might.
Ephesians 6:10 KJV

He Is Strength

The Lord is my strength and my
song; he has become my salvation.
Psalm 118:14

Behold, God is my salvation;
I will trust, and will not be afraid;
for the Lord God is my strength
and my song, and he has
become my salvation.
Isaiah 12:2 RSV

Sing aloud to God our strength;
make a joyful shout to the
God of Jacob.
Psalm 81:1 NKJV

My flesh and my heart fail;
but God is the strength of my heart
and my portion forever.
Psalm 73:26 NKJV

He Gives Strength

You armed me with strength
for battle; you made my
adversaries bow at my feet.
2 Samuel 22:40

It is God that girdeth me with
strength, and maketh
my way perfect.
Psalm 18:32 KJV

He giveth power to the faint;
and to them that have no might
he increaseth strength.
Isaiah 40:29 KJV

God's Little Book of Promises

The Truth about Stress

You will keep in perfect peace
him whose mind is steadfast,
because he trusts in you. Trust in
the Lord forever, for the Lord,
the Lord, is the Rock eternal.
Isaiah 26:3-4

Come to Me, all you who
labor and are heavy laden,
and I will give you rest.
Matthew 11:28 NKJV

May the Lord of peace himself
give you peace at all times
and in every way.
2 Thessalonians 3:16

Moreover, when God gives
any man wealth and possessions,
and enables him to enjoy them,
to accept his lot and be happy in
his work—this is a gift of God.
Ecclesiastes 5:19

Finding Peace

I will listen to what God the Lord
will say; he promises peace
to his people, his saints.
Psalm 85:8

Great peace have they which love thy
law: and nothing shall offend them.
Psalm 119:165 KJV

Therefore being justified by faith,
we have peace with God through
our Lord Jesus Christ.
Romans 5:1 KJV

And let the peace of God rule in
your hearts, to the which
also ye are called in one body;
and be ye thankful.
Colossians 3:15 KJV

Godly Peace

Lord, you will establish peace for us,
for You have also done
all our works in us.
Isaiah 26:12 NKJV

Consider the blameless,
observe the upright; there is a
future for the man of peace.
Psalm 37:37

Those who trust in the Lord
are like Mount Zion, which cannot
be moved, but abides forever.
Psalm 125:1 NKJV

"And in this place I will grant peace,"
declares the Lord Almighty.
Haggai 2:9

And the peace of God, which
passeth all understanding,
shall keep your hearts and minds
through Christ Jesus.
Philippians 4:7 KJV

God's Little Book of Promises

The Truth about Success

True humility and respect for the Lord
lead a man to riches,
honor and long life.
Proverbs 22:4 TLB

And, of course, it is very good
if a man has received wealth from
the Lord, and the good health
to enjoy it. To enjoy your work and
to accept your lot in life—that is
indeed a gift from God.
Ecclesiastes 5:19 TLB

You will decide on a matter,
and it will be established for you,
and light will shine on your ways.
Job 22:28 RSV

Riches and honor are with me,
enduring wealth and prosperity. My
fruit is better than gold, even fine
gold, and my yield than choice silver.
Proverbs 8:18-19 RSV

Heavenly Success

He should eat and drink and
enjoy the fruits of his labors,
for these are gifts from God.
Ecclesiastes 3:13 TLB

Wealth and riches are in his house,
and his righteousness endures forever.
Psalm 112:3

Beloved, I pray that you may prosper
in all things and be in health,
just as your soul prospers.
3 John 2 NKJV

In My Father's house are many
dwelling places; if it were not so,
I would have told you; for I go
to prepare a place for you. And if
I go and prepare a place for you,
I will come again, and receive you
to Myself; that where I am,
there you may be also.
John 14:2-3 NASB

Success on Earth

The Lord your God will make
you abound in all the work of
your hand, in the fruit of your body,
in the increase of your livestock,
and in the produce of your
land for good.
Deuteronomy 30:9 NKJV

Blessed is every one who fears the
Lord, who walks in His ways.
When you eat the labor of your
hands, you shall be happy,
and it shall be well with you.
Psalm 128:1-2 NKJV

He shall be like a tree planted by
the rivers of water, that brings forth
its fruit in its season, whose leaf
also shall not wither; and
whatever he does shall prosper.
Psalm 1:3 NKJV

The Truth about Suffering

He is despised and rejected by men,
a Man of sorrows and acquainted
with grief. And we hid, as it
were, our faces from Him;
He was despised, and we
did not esteem Him.
Isaiah 53:3 NKJV

He then began to teach them
that the Son of Man must suffer
many things and be rejected by the
elders, chief priests and teachers of
the law, and that he must be killed
and after three days rise again.
Mark 8:31

How To Handle Suffering

That is why, for Christ's sake,
I delight in weaknesses, in insults,
in hardships, in persecutions,
in difficulties. For when
I am weak, then I am strong.
2 Corinthians 12:10

For I consider that the sufferings of
this present time are not worthy to be
compared with the glory which shall
be revealed in us.
Romans 8:18 NKJV

Thou therefore endure hardness,
as a good soldier of Jesus Christ.
2 Timothy 2:3 KJV

For to you it has been granted
on behalf of Christ, not only
to believe in Him, but also
to suffer for His sake.
Philippians 1:29 NKJV

173

Triumph over Suffering

A righteous man may have
many troubles, but the Lord
delivers him from them all.
Psalm 34:19

Blessed is the man who endures
temptation; for when he has been
proved, he will receive the crown
of life which the Lord has promised
to those who love Him.
James 1:12 NKJV

Because he himself suffered when
he was tempted, he is able to help
those who are being tempted.
Hebrews 2:18

Share with me in the sufferings
for the gospel according to the
power of God, who has saved us
and called us with a holy calling,
not according to our works, but
according to His own purpose and
grace which was given to us in
Christ Jesus before time began.
2 Timothy 1:8-9 NKJV

The Truth about Temptation

Put on the whole armor of God,
that you may be able to stand
against the wiles of the devil.
Ephesians 6:11 NKJV

Be self-controlled and alert.
Your enemy the devil prowls around
like a roaring lion looking for
someone to devour.
1 Peter 5:8

The Lord knows how to deliver
the godly out of temptations and to
reserve the unjust under punishment
for the day of judgment.
2 Peter 2:9 NKJV

Watch and pray so that you will not
fall into temptation. The spirit is
willing, but the body is weak.
Mark 14:38

Help from God

No temptation has overtaken you
that is not common to man. God is
faithful, and he will not let you be
tempted beyond your strength,
but with the temptation will
also provide the way of escape,
that you may be able to endure it.
1 Corinthians 10:13 RSV

For since he himself has now been
through suffering and temptation,
he knows what it is like when we
suffer and are tempted, and he is
wonderfully able to help us.
Hebrews 2:18 TLB

You are of God, little children,
and have overcome them, because
He who is in you is greater than
he who is in the world.
1 John 4:4 NKJV